44 Thorns in My Heart

Jana Colby

Copyright 2025 Jana Colby

ISBN: 979-8-218-81921-7

44 Thorns in My Heart

After I Die 1
Bad Man 2
Cemetery Dance 3
Chameleon 4
Cover Me 5
Curtain 6
Evil 7
I Live 8
I Made Up My Mind 9
Imagine 10
Intuition 11
Jealous 12
Karma 13
Last Call 14
Letter 15
Living 16
Maple Leaves 17
Masquerade 18
Misery 19
My Best Friend 20
Never here... 21
Nothing is Real 22
O God 23
Ocean 24
Patience 25
Pleading 26
Please Stop 27
Power 28
Sanity 29
Shallow 30

Snake	31
Standing	32
Strong	33
Taken	34
The Fly	35
The House	36
The Light	37
The Train	38
Ticking	39
True Justice	40
Visit	41
Who	42
Will You?	43
You are nothing	44

After I Die

After I die I will learn
reason for pain and sanctity,
what I have missed in a gone world…
goodness and prosperity.

After I die I will know
who was my real enemy
who secretly wished me plunge
into a hole of demony

After I die I will see
where my eyes were blind before
clouded pictures become clear
there will be no more doubt

After I die
from above maybe I can do
great things I have planned
but not to grant…on earth…

Bad Man

I want to talk to you
bad man, awful spirit
you are gone now, forever and
I have sooo many questions for you...

How did it feel to die alone?
What went thru your head
when life was leaving your veins?

Did you feel cries of people you hurt?
did you feel pain you caused?

Do you hear wicked souls
hissing and kicking now?

How does it feel, big hero,
rusting so many lives?

Time won't turn back for the redemption
you're longing for so bad

It is final as you know now
What did you say?

I can't hear your answer,
not even mumbling
swamps of hell are not letting you talk,
not letting you breath, not letting you be.

How does it feel?

Cemetery Dance

Drowsy music is swinging my hips
tiny waist without competition
the onlooker Moon, the only one
gentle caressing my face

So easy to move thru crosses
not even a tear on lace
bony feet stirring grass floor
nothing is in the way

Melody of heart, no aching
genius composer notes
no human can stop me from shining
peeling off tainted coats

I can dance till the morning
not waking a single soul
putting behind all worries
living in a justly world

Free... at last!

Chameleon

How tricky you think you are?
I can see inside of you
false smile and empty promises
you are so poor inside

Changing colors in endless seasons
sleek creations of a sick mind
luring promises hidden in riddles
with intention to make me blind

Your charm is devil's chime
singing melody of madness
which takes me to euphoria
always ending in sadness

The vision I see is not real
playing with my sanity
just unlock your vile heart
to show some humanity

Cover Me

I want to sneak inside
past alluring gate
take a peak of some
sweet living

Just don't crush me now
I am trying hard
to stop bleeding

Be on my site
for a little while
until I shake off
bad feelings

Help me get through ache
coat me in strong fate
to enjoy being

Cover me!

Curtain

Losing myself on the stage of history
curtain is up and I play the role

I do not hear whispers correcting my lines
I do not like how I sound

Forcefully babbling line by line
drowning in torment of unknown

My body is weak and I can't stand
no one is giving me a hand

Trying to figure out how to cheat lines
of my glum and confused play

Oh I am bad actor... I can't act
feeling more like a clown

Who is going to clap for me
when the curtain falls down?

You???

Evil

I met an evil in a form of she
I never agreed with God on this
and then the day of mishap came
it took a while to know her game

It sickens me just to hear her name
charcoal heart with rotten veins
dazzled with green loot
attention seeking...thinking gain

Like a true evil it blinded all
so-called... family ties…
snatching gold, leaving dirt
and mouth full of slime

Only evil can never stop
nagging for years and years
spitting sulfer all around
only her canny worms are dear

Can't you see God?
Can you ?

I Live

I am so happy to come back
to the place of my dreams,
drawn to mystery
which other people fear

Where they find death
I find life,
beautiful things,
names with real meanings

Everyone is remembered
in a shade of swaying leaves,
golden letters,
and broken angel wings

Every tombstone
has a life clouded to livings...
web of destinies
lies in the front of me

I want to know it all.
who to pick? where to start?
inviting callings
with stories to tell

Feeling so close to them,
spending my lifetime listening
I love it because I belong here
I really do!

I Made Up My Mind

I made up my mind
to go to your place in the mountains,
where my love touches God's Eden

Falling snowflakes glittered like diamonds
in the dream, making me dizzy
leading me to breathless ecstasy

Time went by so fast
in a turmoil of feelings, head spinning words
sweet like honey in frozen dew

I asked myself, do I deserve this heaven on earth?
But there was no answer, just a breeze of fresh air
filling me with pleasures

And now I have to leave
the place I love the most
with roses turning into thorns in my heart

and every step I go away
they pierce deeper and deeper
leaving me in sweet red agony

Imagine

Imagine human...imagine
that one day you will be gone
sooner or later
no more thrill no more fun

Hard to hear words of sadness
gliding like a knife thru your heart
when do you stop all this madness
which possesses you now?

Just stop and see, look into yourself
amassed fortune what an illusion
Pretense smile? Nonsense clapping?
World's falsest ovations....

Look around, see the needs
let them speak to you
so the day you go will be filled
with sunny adieu...

Intuition

Born in a shadow of waterfall intuition
no one can see me thru the mist,
ignoring outlines of faint silhouette
humans are busy with tainted things

And waterfall falls and never stops falling
endless mist dying and reviving
people will drown you in poisonous drops
calling it... living...

Climbing up on slimy stones
slipping off and crushing my bod
ignored screams for help...
purpose is served...

The bruises are real, so are broken bones
echoes for help is fading
feeling poor bones and flesh
no one is aiding...

Just timeless little bug is there
in your beaten head telling you
stay awake!

Listen to your intuition!

Jealous

Your house is a cold stone,
with purple flowers smiling at the world
Mine is so frosty despite sun shining

Your soul is in peace now
mine is screaming in desperation
to get to your place....

Jealous of your calm, flying in the air
while I must count painful steps in my destiny

You have it easy, no waking up to dire hours,
no burden of this world's troubles.

Oh how I live in a dark place
without sparks... anywhere
and yours?

It is like a sunray flickering every second
so clean and pure... cherubs nest

Yours eyes are freed and mine have to stay open
to see all unfairness in this word

Where will I find the strength to crawl
thru empty words and countless lies?

Oh how jealous I am of you, for not living...

Karma

Oh karma, karma!
Sneaky is your other name,
which some of us think is fictitious
spying on us from endless corners
let us play a hero a bit…
so you can squeeze hard later,
laughing at us, how we gasp for air
like an unexpected twister rising, rippling,
just enough to see all the anguish we cost
chink, chink some of us still do not get it
lying to ourselves, honesty is gone,
devil is telling you, oh no you are great…
but things are happening
belief is confusing, fear starts to grow
everything is falling around you,
hand is pulling you up
claw is yanking you down
karma karma you are right,
nobody escapes you in any way
we are your puppets
and you are the master of pulling strings
whichever direction
especially where we do not want to go
escaping is not in your dictionary
the bigger the sin the deeper it hurts
so we suffer more
chink, chink watch your life
and better believe in me……

Karma!!!

Last Call

Waiting in a scare
you know it's coming
but you do not dare
to hear, to think,
everything is slow, stiff
no sleep just a numbness
in an empty stare

Yes you care you care
like never before
but it's too late
nothing can stitch
that awful tear

And then it comes
ruthless ring
with shaking hands
picking up
do not want to hear
the words
but I have to...

Everything ended
at 3:56 am

Letter

Writing you a letter
which you can't read
with eyes closed
you can't see it

shimmer of eyelashes
is long time gone
lips are sealed
without sweet calm

frantically chaining
salty confessions
hoping for revival
of blown chances

Too late, too late
for a deep bounds,
hug-less infinity
under dusty ground

maybe just maybe
you are near me

maybe just maybe
you can hear me...

Living

People live
like they would live forever
grabbing things
thinking they are clever

They cheat themselves
with shiny little things
huge lands
and houses worthy of kings

And years fly by
choices are made
good or bad
prices are paid

The real truth
is getting scary
the closer it gets
it makes us worry

What will happen
when facing your death?
What will matter
when taking your last breath?

Maple Leaves

Maple leaves kissing ground
It is that time of the year
expecting changing shades
just see one...

They can't rest
Just moan there
all... being crushed
without aching

Mud is starting
to shape colors
to horrific dirty

Denting and chipping off
gentle glaze of want
ripping up all leaves
until maple dreams disappear

Hm.......???

Masquerade

Whole word is a masquerade
masks created by feelings
and ugly human desires
hiding behind second faces

Masquerade of mish mash
secret moves in unsolved riddles
catastrophes from hurt egos
clustered wishes so nasty and wrong
were they really created by God?

Only humans can be so wicked
changing masks with weather
so unpredictable and rotten
frozen and hot
destroying everything
will the cleansing ever come?

Hm, I hope so.....

Misery

One day I forgot to close the door
and misery came in without knocking

I didn't really notice why I was in spleen,
she was running thru my house laughing

She went to work fast spreading unhappiness
feeding from a bowl of tears

She truly did destroyed everything
and all of it was based on fears

I tried to catch her but she is smart
hiding in a cracks of walls

How can I get her out of here
without leaving ugly scars?

My Best Friend

You always hold my hand
walking me thru mud
watching all my odds
saving me from blood

You heal my every step
which I slowly take
when bottom of my soul
is crying for a break

You wipe my every tear
and listen to my heart
work on big ideas
giving me a fresh start

You know my every move
you feel my every breath
you are always with me
till my lonely death

My best friend... the pen

Never here...

I was never here
or was I?
Who would know?
Who would notice?
Maybe someone did
for a while for a sec
for their selfish desires
to do, to use,
chores and chores
non-existent joy
crushed spirit
piling problems
no way out,
just prayers and anger
tiredness,
no changes
leaves kept falling and falling
only two seasons were changing
last winter was fatal
icy flurry took me away
somewhere,
nothing changed
time for next...
I was never here
Or was I?

Nothing is Real

Nothing is real in a real world
having no clue what to do
how to outshine the sun
what to do in a blow

Brain is full of saggy thoughts
help is nowhere to find
confusion rises up fast
how can I fight with plots?

Shivering standing in gale
hail falling on me
tearing my flesh pale
the only one I have

Nothing is real in a real world
nothing at all I know now...

O God

O God, forgive the poor souls
who don't want to live in this world
who want to live in fantasy
where all good things happen

Wishing for years to go faster
tired of praying eyes and nagging words
grief needles soaked in pain
poking the veins of their life

Just peace and quiet they want
not much just dream with sun
watch the flowers to grow
and never be on run...

O God, forgive the poor souls
for thinking the way you don't
please, help to lift your children
or leave them in darkness, doomed

All will be the way you want !

Ocean

Yes, I can cry in the ocean
hidden from everyone
where no one is judging
joyless spirit from this earth...

Only there I feel free to chat,
to sunken shipyards and treasures,
embracing finality

Lost coins are the sole light
in the sadness of my mind

Yes, I can cry in the ocean
full of mysteries
hidden in deep waters
forever stranded...

With passing time
blue and my tears become one
gentle, never asking... why?

Leaving me with just one wish
of changing into a mermaid,
disappearing into the solitude of the ocean
where everyone cares...

Patience

Do not be scared my dear
waves of despair brought you here
there is a purpose for this change
just stay calm and think

It will take awhile for you to agree
with all added hurts
but slowly you can get there
to understand why, to be

Slipping is not the option
even when going thru flames
God has its own ways
to dry your tears with caution

Do not be sad my brave hero
nothing in world is ideal
I already see a winning glow
above your heavy ordeal

Patience...

Pleading

Pleading, begging every day
heart's bloodcurdling screams
no one listens and they can't
the only truth is near

Thinning paper is rolling out fast
with stories written by life
hard to read some of them
what happened in the past

So much anguish
with little cheer
protruding like scars
in smeared letters nothing is clear
everything happened too fast

Luring the time
with gold and riches
bribe-less ignorance, no answers
looking to find some glitches
in its thick skin of panzer

No success...
Please life… turn back

Please Stop

Please, stop the light
from calling me back
my work is not done yet

In shadow of death
I only began
fulfilling my true callings

Just now just now
in autumn years
with winter quickly approaching
I see sunrise at sundown
and glorious glare in the dark

From cheerless existence
soaring ideas
make roads to endless skies
brain working at lighting speed
taking memories to new heights

Now I can reach
what I could not before
with all my broken soul

Just please, stop the light
from calling me back

My life has just begun!

Power

I fear soooo thee
how with one move
you can destroy everything
your power is beyond all

Crushing awkward theories
I have had about breathing
in this world

Your plans are clever
there is no comparison
all big heads can only nod
in distress, of never...

There is no question
who is higher,
so simple ,yet so complicated

Just bow your head
in front of thee
because you can never win!

Sanity

Sanity, Dear
what makes you whole?
callow puff?
or lion's roar?

Show me your true face
what does make sense?

Time changes preferences
shifting from happy to pain
creating an endless game?

Pokes of misery in my body
undecided moves
finishing line
you can't reach,
just can't find that switch

Brain is sucked out dry
shrinking with running time
how can I fulfill your needs?
How can you help me live?

Shallow

Who is going to save me now?
Now in my old age?
Now in my forgotten youth?

Who will show mercy
to old me? Forgotten?
Sacrificing everything?

World is looking
for endless youth and beauty
What about me?
I am nobody... lost in no land
yet breathing

Nobody cares, so sad
Nobody appreciates
Worst torture of life

They all want now...
Now and now....
Beautiful faces and visions,
not reality... or is it???

So shallow? I guess yes
No echo of mercy

Now I have to live in my shell...

Like nobody

Crying...

Snake

Oh, that snake is after you
getting under your skin
can't you see his scaly body
in the filthy field?

Winding his road to your heart
like termites in wood
it is not hard to understand
what's hiding under the hood

Growing pressure from his tracks
forcing you to do
things you would never do before
without feeling blue

With melding marks you become one
and madness starts to grow
evil urges and intentions
tears began to flow

Is there a way back?

Standing

Standing in a cold night
looking at the black sight

Hair-raising sounds like wet chains
nearing echoes of knocking cane

Eerie feeling came over me
I can't stay nor can I flee

It is getting closer and I can't move
my head is buzzing in weird mood

My feet are glued to the ground
and I hear nothing but beastly sounds

It started to torture me with cold hands
I am all frozen, that's how it gets

And then I burst into hot flames
feeling so sorry for all the shames

Is that conscience???

Strong

I see beautiful visions
in the air
uplifting like a sweet breeze

I close my eyes
and let myself be taken
in greatness of universe

Naive but not ashamed
feeling what others disdain,
because that is the only true
which stays with you

When you are alone
with your thoughts
and nobody can take it away

Just go ahead
feel who you are
despite odd feelings, all is good!

Taken

It started with a whisper
and she was taken in
little did she know
he was only sin

Fluffy words full of admiration
glazed with honey,
and fatal fixation

Luring snap and bird was caged

Powerful latch
wasn't a fair match
for feathery being

Chilly steel
from crisscrossed clink
caused beak to shut
in a bitter blink

Drowning the heart
in endless tears
drop by drop hope fades

Oh... it hurts,
but justice is there
which no men can touch

Just be aware birdie, be aware!

The Fly

Do not kill the little fly on the wall
she wants to live, but why?
With all annoying questions
buzzing around...
yet, your only sweet ally
in this evil world
there are two of you, scared,
painful heartbeats eroding wits
in lightheaded cruel days
trying to survive...
blistered lips from endless litany
friends are gone,
mastering hurtful tricks
naive thirst for honest game,
shhh...... just listen
maybe your luck will change,
shut your eyes in a wish…
sleep on imaginary clouds
away from reality... for now,
just do not kill the little fly on the wall
think, before you hit the wall...

The House

Step into the house where no one thrives
vain draft dragging you thru corridors
stroking silver door knobs of sad rooms
nothing to see and admire

Rainbow pressed hard into dirty carpets
sobbing walls ringing in ears
no great mastery was brewed here

Creatures of magic disappeared
butterfly wings weighed down by filth
layers of change stay unpeeled

Grounds are shaking
house is sinking,
run, run before it falls
before you perish in foolish ruins

Welcome to your house!

The Light

It is the light which hurts my eyes the most
cheerful rays... teasing
skillful birds flying in the skies
shooting down to feed on weak
savaging God's creations
is this the real world?

Wherever you go, you can't hide
pointing fingers are everywhere
dragging you out of the safety net
killing you in the web of must...

And there is a light that sinless light
fiercely shining
like it is all right
How can this be? Is it real?
Or is it devilish play to be?

It is the light which hurts my eyes the most,
begging for darkness...

It is the light… which hurts the most
or is it me?

The Train

Black cloud above me
dancing in a weird trance
wherever I move he is there
changing shapes in vain

Riding cursed train
of despair and distractions
vision of light
is more foggy than bright

Cabins packed with sly entities
just a few angels squeezed in between
some get off sooner than you wish
usually the ones with golden sheen

Food is bland and road is crooked
turning stomach from things I see
no mercy pause for runaway train
no help for tormented souls

Sitting stiff, counting my agonies
dreaming about sweet stops
losing myself in choo choo melodies
waiting for a final destination... dead end!

Ticking

Ticking and ticking
away everything

Merciless minutes
biting off
poor and dim existence
as well as riches

In panic pace can't sustain,
digging in madness
can't penetrate shell
of long yearned eternity

Emotions are mounting
anger is rising
power is losing shine of magic

There is no hope
for furious attempts
trying to stop tick

Ticking and ticking...

True Justice

We can't run away
from annoying bony fingers
rattles in white shroud
just inches from us, forever...

Tiptoeing around all the time
from seconds or rise to decades...
leaving no place to hide
no place to take a rest

Dying since birth
irked by unanswered prayers
falling and rising like a star
peeling all those layers

Nobody is chosen
to miss the stop sign
nobody is chosen
to cheat the death

True justice...

Visit

I get a visit from a crow every night
hiding in an old tree from others' sight

He is looking straight into my eyes
and I just can't wait for that moment to pass

Bringing dark thoughts over and over
what I have done to deserve this honor?

I do not want to play this creepy game
but he is luring me in, again and again

I wish to send him to his own world
but I can't force myself to speak a word

One night I will get out of his curse
and light in the morning will create a new verse

Who

Who is it?
Does someone care?
Passing by and no eye
no touch, no word
so many of you out there
unknown, unloved, sad?

Are you one of many tears
which freely flow to rivers?
Which people hate
and do not want to bother?

In the ditch spit on and run over,
shivering in cold, in hunger?
With hurt your only friend?
With stones your only food?

Who is going to see you
thru tears in your eyes
thru tape on your mouth?
Is someone going to lift you up
and wash your face in mercy?

Who is it?
Do you care?

Will You?

Will you care for me
when sickness and old age
will sallow my skin
and unbearable pain
will torture me like a dark sin?

Will you feed me bread
when no mouth be there
cursed from saying truth
and I can't say a word
will your love be crushed?

When no move is there
from my rancid flesh
without finding legs
touching the empty place?

When my beauty sheen
will fizzle in abyss
turning to disgust
choking on stale air
oozing icky puss?

Will you care for me?

You are nothing

You are nothing...
your ego is in the way,
soooo… cocky and proud of what?

Ripping people lives apart to justify
so called truth and power of yours?
Are you proud of pain and suffering?

You are nothing just bad smelling dust
which wants to fall over weakness
is that your measure?

Poor is your soul,
frying on satanic altar

Be proud of good you can do,
fine change and grace

Your measure is the devil's measure
don't you see what matters?

You are nothing without duty to good
nothing without saving lives all kinds

Nothing without passion for justice
just flesh and bones glued together.

You just nothing, nothing and nothing
You want to change???

www.ingramcontent.com/pod-product-compliance
Lightning Source LLC
Chambersburg PA
CBHW022126040426
42450CB00006B/862